MARY JOE FERNANDEZ

A Real-Life Reader Biography

Melanie Cole

Mitchell Lane Publishers, Inc.
P.O. Box 200 • Childs, Maryland 21916

Copyright © 1998 by Mitchell Lane Publishers. All rights reserved. No part of this book may be reproduced without written permission from the publisher. Printed and bound in the United States of America.

Second Printing

Real-Life Reader Biographies

Selena	Robert Rodriguez	Mariah Carey	Rafael Palmeiro
Tommy Nuñez	Trent Dimas	Cristina Saralegui	Andres Galarraga
Oscar De La Hoya	Gloria Estefan	Jimmy Smits	**Mary Joe Fernandez**
Cesar Chavez	Chuck Norris	Sinbad	Paula Abdul
Vanessa Williams	Celine Dion	Mia Hamm	Sammy Sosa
Brandy	Michelle Kwan	Rosie O'Donnell	Shania Twain
Garth Brooks	Jeff Gordon	Mark McGwire	Salma Hayek
Sheila E.	Hollywood Hogan	Ricky Martin	Britney Spears
Arnold Schwarzenegger	Jennifer Lopez	Kobe Bryant	Derek Jeter
Steve Jobs	Sandra Bullock	Julia Roberts	Robin Williams
Jennifer Love Hewitt	Keri Russell	Sarah Michelle Gellar	Liv Tyler
Melissa Joan Hart	Drew Barrymore	Alicia Silverstone	Katie Holmes
Winona Ryder	Alyssa Milano		

Library of Congress Cataloging-in-Publication Data
Cole, Melanie, 1957–
  Mary Joe Fernandez / Melanie Cole.
    p. cm.—(A real-life reader biography)
  Includes index.
  Summary: Profiles the life of this Hispanic tennis player who went pro as a teenager, continued her schooling, and has become one of the top ranked women players in the world.
  ISBN 1-883845-63-7
  1. Fernandez, Mary Joe, 1971– —Juvenile literature. 2. Tennis players—United States—Biography—Juvenile literature. 3. Women tennis players—United States—Biography—Juvenile literature. [1. Fernandez, Mary Joe, 1971– . 2. Tennis players. 3. Hispanic Americans—Biography. 4. Women—Biography.] I. Title. II. Series.
GV994.F47C65 1998
796.342′092—dc21   97-43510
[B]   CIP
                                                                                                AC

ABOUT THE AUTHOR: Melanie Cole has been a writer and editor for seventeen years. She was previously an associate editor of *Texas Monthly* and is now managing editor of *Hispanic* magazine. She has published numerous poems, articles, and reviews in various journals, magazines, and newspapers. She is also a contributing writer to the Mitchell Lane series **Famous People of Hispanic Heritage.** A native of Kansas, Ms. Cole now resides in Austin, Texas.
PHOTO CREDITS: cover courtesy T-V Enterprises Ltd.; p. 4 sketch by Barbara Tidman; p. 71 courtesy T-V Enterprises Ltd.; p. 12 AP Photo/Elise Amendola; p. 15 Archive Photos; p. 19 Globe Photos; p. 20 AP Photo/Franz Neumayr; p. 22 Reuters/Corbis-Bettmann; p. 24 Reuters/Corbis-Bettmann; p. 26 AP Photo/Elise Amendola; p. 28 AP Photo/Steve Holland; p. 30 courtesy T-V Enterprises Ltd.
ACKNOWLEDGMENTS: The following story has been thoroughly researched and checked for accuracy. To the best of our knowledge, it represents a true story. This story is not authorized by Mary Joe Fernandez.

Table of Contents

Chapter 1   Tennis Toddler 5

Chapter 2   Champion in School 10

Chapter 3   Champion on the Court 16

Chapter 4   Olympic Glory 21

Chapter 5   Tough Yet Tender 27

Chronology 32

Index 32

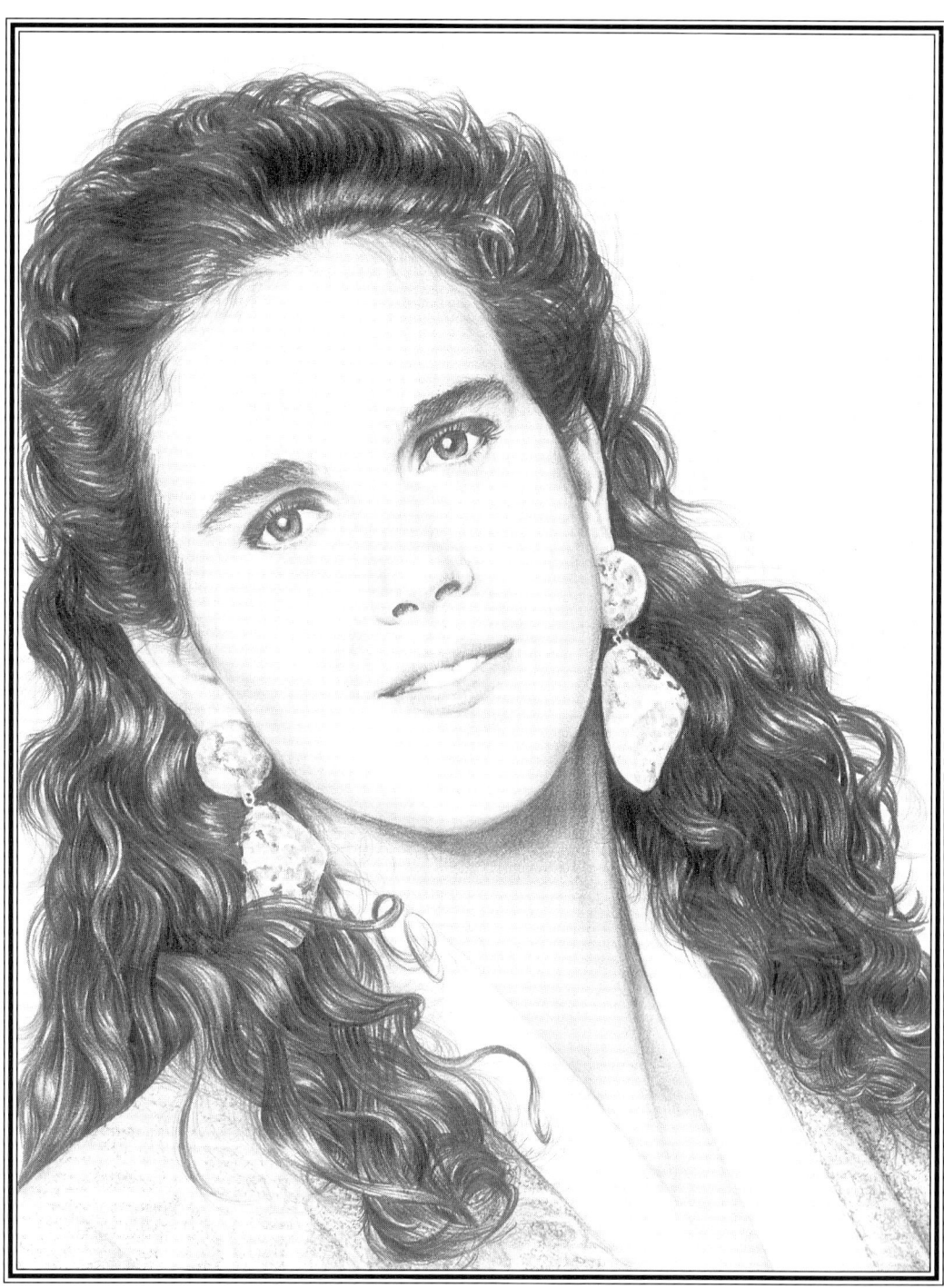

Chapter 1
Tennis Toddler

Little Mary Joe wanted to play tennis like her older sister, Mimi. So Mary Joe's father, José, let her tag along when he took Mimi to the court to practice. He took an old wooden racket and cut it down to fit her tiny hand. With her special racket, she loved to bounce tennis balls off the wall. Two years later, she started taking tennis lessons.

José saw how much his three-year-old daughter loved her special racket. He and Mary Joe's mother,

When Mary Joe was a little girl, she loved to bounce tennis balls off the wall.

When Mary Joe was five years old, her father knew she had a talent for tennis.

Silvia, let her play tennis whenever she wanted. When Mary Joe was five, her father asked a tennis champion to watch her play. The champion told José that Mary Joe was talented. He advised José to start her in tennis lessons and to enter her in as many tournaments (contests) as possible.

The name Mary Joe is the English version of the Spanish name Maria José. Mary Joe was born on August 19, 1971, in the Dominican Republic. Her parents gave her her father's name for a middle name. Mary Joe's parents met in Havana, Cuba. They were married there. But when Fidel Castro and his Revolutionary Army took over Cuba in 1959, the couple escaped to the Dominican Republic. Both Mary Joe and her sister were born in the Dominican Republic.

When Mary Joe was three months old, the family decided to move to the United States. They settled in Miami, Florida.

When Mary Joe was in elementary school, her tennis coaches talked to her parents about entering her in amateur tournaments. These tournaments are sponsored by the United States Tennis Association (USTA). They are grouped by age bracket, but the youngest bracket is the "twelves." If young players are really good, they can play even if they are younger than twelve. Mary Joe won the USTA Nationals title in the twelves bracket at the age of ten.

From age eleven to fourteen, Mary Joe won four singles USTA championships. These tournaments were held each year at the Orange Bowl in her hometown of Miami.

She won several tennis tournaments before she was out of elementary school.

She was the first girl ever to win so many back-to-back titles. Each time she won, she was younger than the age division in which she competed. At eleven, she again won the title for players twelve and under. At thirteen, she won the sixteens title. And the next year, at fourteen, she won the championship for girls eighteen and under.

Mary Joe was a champion tennis player before she was a teenager.

Chapter 2
Champion in School

Mary Joe decided to turn pro when she was just fourteen years old.

Mary Joe played in her first professional (pro) tournament when she was thirteen. She participated as an amateur. She beat her first opponent, a 33-year-old woman. That same year, she defeated the eleventh-ranked player in the world.

As Mary Joe became a better and better player, she had to make a big decision. She had been playing in the amateur junior circuit. With her family's support, she decided to turn pro at the age of fourteen. This decision meant that she could earn money, but it brought another kind of pressure. Agents, fellow players, and fans began saying she should drop out of school. Many other players did this. But Mary Joe did not drop out. She wanted to go to Carrollton School of the Sacred Heart and play tennis on the side. She had made up her mind, and her parents supported her.

It is sad that many young tennis players do drop out of school. They do this so that they can earn more money and have a longer tennis career. More often than not, the girls never finish their studies. They focus solely on the sport. Their parents sometimes push the girls to win and make more money. Players as different as

She did not drop out of school, however. She wanted to finish her education and play tennis, too.

Monica Seles, Mary Pierce, and Jennifer Capriati have been pushed by their parents.

Mary Joe says she never received this kind of pressure from her father or mother. Instead, her parents said she should worry about school first and tennis second. She worked her tennis tournaments around her classes. "If Mary Joe doesn't want to study, we make her study," her father said. But, he added, "If she doesn't want to play tennis, we don't make Mary Joe play."

Not only did she stay in school, she tried hard to do well. "I just decided that if I was going to go to school, I was going to do it right," she said. During high school Mary Joe maintained an A average. She did this while earning more than $500,000 in prize money from

During high school, she maintained an A average. She worked her tournaments around her classes.

> **Mary Joe was playing in the French Open when her class graduated from high school. She was allowed to graduate that August.**

tennis. Sometimes she had to miss class to play in a tournament. Her friends would read their class notes to her over the phone so that she could keep up. Sometimes they faxed her their notes.

Her class graduated from Carrollton in 1989. Mary Joe didn't get to walk down the aisle with her class because she was playing in the French Open. She was allowed to take her final exams in August of her senior year. She graduated with honors in August 1989.

To the rest of the world, Mary Joe became known as the player "who finished school." Once a reporter asked her what she thought about young kids turning pro. She replied, "Everybody's different, and everybody matures at a different time—mentally and physically. So it's hard to say at what age it's right or wrong for a person to turn pro. What I would say, though, is that you should finish school first, because there's always time to play tennis afterward, and an education balances out your life. . . . If you have your education, you've got something to fall back on."

Mary Joe concentrates in the semifinals at the Australian Open in 1995.

Chapter 3
Champion on the Court

Mary Joe became the youngest player to win a match in the U.S. Open.

Soon after Mary Joe turned pro, she became the youngest player to win a match in the U.S. Open. But it was only one match. She lost the second match to one of her tennis idols, Chris Evert. In her first full season as a professional, she won 40 of 50 singles matches and two tournaments. She earned more than $1 million. Mary Joe was on her way to becoming a tennis star.

In tennis, the major tournaments—such as the French Open, the U.S. Open, and Wimbledon—are called Grand Slams. Mary Joe reached her first Grand Slam singles final in 1990 at the Australian Open but lost to Steffi Graf in a close match. By February she had made it into the top ten but had not yet won a pro title. She landed her first pro championship at the Tokyo Indoors in September 1990.

The road to her first professional championship was rough. In the Tokyo tournament, she won a three-hour match in a hot indoor gym. Afterward, her stomach muscles began to cramp. She had to have them packed in ice. She had never experienced such pain. Even so, the next day, she got back on the court, feeling very stiff,

She landed her first pro championship at the Tokyo Indoors in 1990.

> **In late 1990 and early 1991, Mary Joe rose from seventh in the world to fourth among all women tennis players.**

and won the title. She celebrated her first professional championship by sleeping for twelve hours.

During the rest of that season, Mary Joe continued to suffer several kinds of injuries. Looking back, she believes it was because she wasn't in top condition due to her part-time schedule during school. She hired a strength coach and started lifting weights to improve her upper body strength. Up until this point, tennis had been her only form of exercise. To be able to compete with the best players, she needed to get much stronger.

In late 1990 and early 1991, Mary Joe rose from seventh in the world to fourth among all women tennis players. This was her highest ranking ever. She was the highest-ranked American other than Martina Navratilova and Chris

Evert since 1980. In 1992, she reached the semis in the U.S. Open singles before losing to Monica Seles.

In recent years, Mary Joe has shown that she is a strong player. She holds six singles titles in major tournaments, including Indian Wells and Tokyo Indoors. She also holds thirteen doubles titles, including the Australian and European Opens. She always plays in the great tournaments:

Below, Mary Joe played in the semifinals in the U.S. Open singles in 1992.

the U.S. Open, Wimbledon, the Virginia Slims tournaments, the Lufthansa Cup, and the Tokyo, Australian, French, and Italian Opens.

Left to right: Mary Joe, Gigi Fernandez, Jennifer Capriati, and coach Billie Jean King at the Federation Cup tournament, April 1996

Chapter 4
Olympic Glory

By the late 1980s, Mary Joe had become a very good doubles player. In 1992, she went to the Summer Olympics in Barcelona, Spain. There she won the gold medal in doubles with partner Gigi Fernandez (who is not related to Mary Joe). She also won the bronze medal in singles.

Some tennis experts think Mary Joe is much better in doubles than in singles. So far she has won more tournaments in doubles play. She has been successful as a

In 1992, Mary Joe won a gold medal in doubles at the Summer Olympics.

doubles partner with many different types of players, including Zina Garrison, Pam Shriver, Robin White, Gigi Fernandez, and Lindsay Davenport.

Mary Joe's favorite moment was the doubles match in Barcelona in which she and Gigi Fernandez won Olympic gold. This victory meant a lot to her. To win the gold, the pair had to defeat the Spanish doubles pair—Arantxa Sanchez Vicario and Conchita Martínez—in front of the king and queen of Spain. It was a sweet victory for Mary Joe because she had been asked to play for Spain but had refused. "I'm an American," she said. "I could play for Spain, where my father was born, or the Dominican Republic, where I was born. But . . . it would be difficult to play for another country. I am very

She won the Olympic gold with partner Gigi Fernandez.

patriotic." In fact, she had been asked to play in the 1988 Olympics for the Dominican Republic but had said no. She said she would rather represent the United States someday.

Gigi Fernandez (left) and Mary Joe kiss their gold medals after receiving their awards August 8, 1992, for winning the women's doubles in Barcelona, Spain.

After winning both a gold and a bronze at Barcelona, Mary Joe said about the Olympics, "For me, this is one of the biggest things ever. . . . I've won the Australian [Open], but this is bigger. This is huge." Her proud father, José, touched the gold medal his daughter had just won and said, "In America, anything is possible."

In 1996, Mary Joe had just bounced back from a four-year slump when she was asked to compete for the United States in the Olympics again. The highlight of her year was winning her second Olympic gold medal. She and Gigi Fernandez, the same team that won in Barcelona in 1992, won the gold in women's tennis doubles at the 1996 Olympics in Atlanta, Georgia.

Mary Joe is a right-handed player with a two-handed

In 1996, Mary Joe and Gigi won a second Olympic gold medal.

Medal winners from the 1996 Olympics in Atlanta, Georgia, display their awards. Mary Joe (third from left) repeated her gold medal performance.

backhand. She originally played in a style similar to that of Chris Evert, but more timid. She has slowly changed her style of play, adding surprise shots to her game. She makes it hard for opponents to guess which way she'll hit the ball next. The new approach has helped her succeed both in Olympic competition and as a professional.

Chapter 5
Tough Yet Tender

Mary Joe knows being a good role model is important. She supports many causes. In 1993 she contributed a women's tennis scholarship to Florida International University in Miami. In 1994 she became the national spokesperson for the Cities in Schools/Burger King Academy program. It was aimed at preventing kids from dropping out of school. She is involved in several charities, such as Big Brother/Big Sister, the

Mary Joe is a good role model. She supports many causes.

Hunger Project, World Vision Projects, and the Special Olympics.

When Hurricane Andrew hit south Florida in 1992, Mary Joe raised money for the victims of the storm. She organized a charity tennis event to benefit those who had lost their homes. She and other top tennis players got together for an exhibition game. Mary Joe told ticket buyers, "You're not just going to watch a tennis match, you're going to help rebuild a community."

Mary Joe's goal is much the same as it has always been since she picked up a racket. She wants to be the best female tennis player in the world. She has earned more than $4.2 million in tennis, but she is rich in other ways. Mary Joe is kind and caring toward others.

When Hurricane Andrew hit south Florida, Mary Joe organized a charity tennis event to raise money for the victims of the storm.

Mary Joe is a generous, caring person as well as a talented tennis player.

Mary Joe has many years before she'll have to retire. Her role model, Chris Evert, retired at 35 and was fourth in the world when she stepped down. "I'm still young and have a lot more years to play," Mary Joe said.

Mary Joe has thought hard about what she wants to do after she does not play tennis anymore. She has always known how important education is. After she retires from tennis, she wants to be a grade-school teacher. "I would like to get involved with kids," she said, "helping them to read and write. Everyone deserves a chance."

> **When she cannot play tennis anymore, Mary Joe would like to work with kids.**

Chronology

- Born August 19, 1971, in the Dominican Republic; mother: Silvia Pino Fernandez; father José Fernandez
- Started playing tennis at three and taking tennis lessons at five
- From ten to fourteen, won the United States Tennis Association (USTA) Nationals.
- In 1985, at the age of fourteen, joined the Women's Tennis Association (WTA)
- Attended Carrollton School of the Sacred Heart in Miami while playing professional tennis; graduated in 1989
- Won her first pro tournament in Tokyo in 1990
- Won a gold medal in doubles and a bronze medal in singles in the 1992 Olympics in Barcelona, Spain
- Won the Brighton International title in 1995
- Won a gold medal in doubles in the 1996 Olympics in Atlanta, Georgia
- As of 1997, had won six singles titles and thirteen doubles titles

Index

Australian Open 15, 17, 19, 20, 25
birth of 6
Capriati, Jennifer 13, 20
Carrollton School of the Sacred Heart 11, 14
Castro, Fidel 6
charity work 27–30
Davenport, Lindsay 23
Dominican Republic 6, 7, 23, 24
education of 7, 11–15, 31
Evert, Chris 16, 19, 26, 31
Fernandez, Gigi 20, 21, 23, 24, 25
Fernandez, José (father) 5–6, 13, 25
Fernandez, Silvia (mother) 6, 13

first pro tournament 10
French Open 14, 17, 20
Graf, Steffi 17
Indian Wells 19
injuries 18
Martínez, Conchita 23
Navratilova, Martina 19
Olympics 21–26
Seles, Monica 13, 19
Tokyo Indoors 17, 19
United States Tennis Association 7
Vicario, Arantxa Sanchez 23
Wimbledon 17, 20
winnings 15, 16, 29

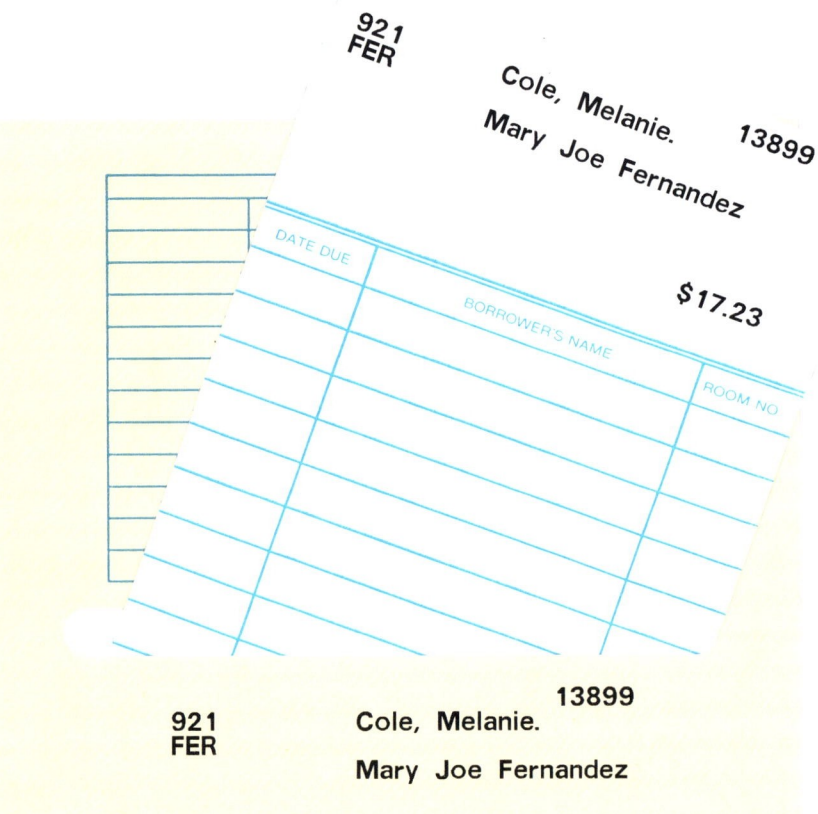

921 Cole, Melanie. 13899
FER
      Mary Joe Fernandez

**LONGFELLOW ELEM SCHOOL
HOUSTON TX 77025**

960859 01723 47724C 47859F   008